Tree-
House
comix
Proudly
Presents

DOG MAN
GRIME AND PUNISHMENT

WRITTEN AND ILLUSTRATED BY **DAV PiLKEY**

AS GEORGE BEARD AND HAROLD HUTCHINS

WITH COLOR BY JOSE GARIBALDI

graphix

AN IMPRINT OF

■SCHOLASTIC

TO AMY BERKOWER, WHO ONCE TOLD ME, "WRITE THE BOOKS THAT MAKE YOU HAPPY." THANK YOU FOR BELIEVING IN ME.

Published in the UK by Scholastic, 2021
Euston House, 24 Eversholt Street, London, NW1 1DB
Scholastic Ireland, 89E Lagan Road, Dublin Industrial Estate,
Glasnevin, Dublin, D11 HP5F

SCHOLASTIC and associated logos are trademarks
and/or registered trademarks of Scholastic Inc.

First published in the US by Scholastic Inc, 2020

Text and illustrations © Dav Pilkey, 2020

The right of Dav Pilkey to be identified as the
author and illustrator of this work has been asserted
by him under the Copyright, Designs and Patents Act 1988.

ISBN 978 0702 31067 6

A CIP catalogue record for this book is available from the British Library.

Printed in China
Paper made from wood grown in sustainable forests
and other controlled sources.

9 10 8

www.scholastic.co.uk

Edited by Ken Geist
Book design by Dav Pilkey and Phil Falco
Colour by Jose Garibaldi
Colour flatting by Aaron Polk
Publisher: David Saylor

CHAPTERS

George and Harold
Celebrities at Large

Intro #1

Hiya, Pals. It's your boys George and Harold!

'Sup?

You're not gonna believe this, but we TOTALLY Got FAMOUS!

It all started last week when we were selling our comics at the mall...

HEY!

Tree HOUSE Comix $2.00

The Geniuses Are IN

You CAN'T Peddle Your WARES here!

COMIX $2.00

The Geniuses Are IN

We're not Peddling wares!!!

Yeah! I've never Peddled a ware in my life!

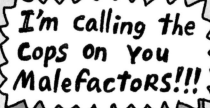

Hey, these comics are **AWESOME!**

Thanks!

We have a special discount for cops!

Yeah! **3** for **5** Bucks!

Okay! I'll take three!

Give me **SIX!!!**

Ka-ching!

zong

AREN'T YOU GONNA ARREST THEM??

Relax, Sherlock! They're just kids!

The cops told everybody about our comics...

TreeHouse Comix $3.50

"Awesome!"
—The cops

...And soon the crowds grew and grew.

Miami Valley MALL

THE Daily NEWS★

MALL is Popular Again

Thanks To Juveniles' Comics!!!

Mall Manager

What should we do about those two Kids?

I Know! Let's Give them free food and stuff!

Mall Manager

ZONG

And so...

eeHouse
mix $5.00

"Juvenile"
—The Daily News

Thanks for the root-beer floats, Sherlock!

MY NAME'S NOT SHERLOCK! I'VE TOLD YA, LIKE, FIFTY TIMES!

Well, we better get started on our next comic!!!

Our Public awaits!

While we work on our next tale of Depth and maturity...

...check out our story thus far!!!

TURN

DOG MAN

our story thus far...

One day a cop and a police Dog...

... got hurt in an explosion!

POP

Wee-ooo-wee-ooo-wee

They GOT rushed to the hospital...

...but the doctor had SAD news:

Boo-Hoo!

Sorry, cop Dude-but your head is dying!

aw, Darn it!!!

And your **BODY** is dying, Doggy dude!

whine whine whine

But then the Nurse Lady got a supa lit idea.

I know! Let's stitch the dog's head onto cop's Body!!!

You're a **Genius**, Nurse Lady!!!

I Know.

So they had a big operation...

...and that's how Dog Man started.

Dog Man Kept the city safe from evildoers...

RATS!

...until one day...

...when everything changed.

Hi, Papa!

Petey, the world's most evil cat...

...was trans- formed by Love...

...And now he's a GOOD GUY!

But even though Petey's **HEART** has changed...

...his **MIND** is still haunted by the Ghosts of his past.

Petey! **I AM YOUR FATHER!**

HEY! This didn't happen!

If Petey is gonna continue to **DO GOOD...**

...he might need a little help from his **FRIENDS!**

I BARELY know these people!

So sit back and enjoy...

...our newest epic **GRAPHIC NOVEL!**

IT'S ONLY A COMIC BOOK!

Isn't he the **ONLY** <u>Chief</u> in town???

Shhh!

Here to present the award...

...is Chief's very **Best Friend**...

...**DOG MAN!**

YAY, CHIEF!

HOORAY! YAY!

CLAP-CLAP CLAP-CLAP-CLAP

YAY, CHIEF!

CHIEF ROCKS! YEAH!

CLAP-CLAP CLAP

YAY, CHIEF!

CLAP

Where is he?

He was just here a minute ago!

I'll bet he's outside digging up those flower beds!!!

MY ROSES!

Aw, Don't worry, Mayor...

...DOG Man would never do anything like that!!!

OH, DOG MAN!

MAYOR'S
Roses
(keep out)

Listen! Here he
comes now!!!

chief

chief

STEP 1.
First, place your left hand inside the dotted lines marked "Left hand here." Hold the book open FLAT!

STEP 2:
Grasp the right-hand page with your thumb and index finger (inside the dotted lines marked "Right Thumb Here").

STEP 3:
Now quickly flip the right-hand page back and forth until the picture appears to be Animated.

(For extra fun, try adding your own sound-effects!)

O-RAMA

REMEMBER,

While you are flipping, be sure you can see the image on page **23** **AND** the image on page **25**.

If you flip quickly, the two pictures will start to look like **ONE** **ANIMATED** cartoon.

Don't forget to add your own sound-effects!!!

Left hand here.

Right
Thumb
here.

26

Don't Cry, Mayor! He was just—

I'M NOT CRYING!!!

He slobbered all over my Glasses...

...he got GRIME all over my new SUIT...

sniff sniff

...And he Dug up MY Rose GARDEN!

City Hall

If that DoG-headed Cop messes up ONE MORE TiME...

... I'm gonna take his **BADGE** Away!!!

Don't Worry, sir. Dog Man just gets excited, that's all!

He'll be Good from now on!

WELL I Should HOPE SO!!!

Now where's my hat?

CHAPTER 2
The Saddest CHAPTER Ever Written

...So you'll always remember us.

Here's the bone that you like to chew.

Here's your squeaky toy telephone...

squeak squeak

...and here's the little ball you love to—

I'm not gonna cry. I'm not gonna—

I'm not gonna—

Lish SPLASH SPlish SPLASH

42

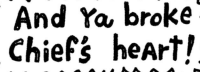

 YOU MADE Everyone CRY!

 And Ya broke Chief's heart!

 Get out of here, DOG MAN! AND DON'T COME BACK!

SPLish SPLish SPLish

COPS

SPLASH!

OW-WOOOO

OW-OW-OWOOOOOOOOOOOOOOOOOOOOO

OW-OWOOOO! OW-OW-OW-OWOOOOOOOOOOOOOOOOOOOO

CHAPTER 3

The Chapter That's Totally Not as Sad as The Last one

Meanwhile...

It's okay, 80-HD...

...You can make the tree red.

It's __our__ story. We can color it any way we want!

Hey, Look! Dog Man is home from—

What's wrong, Dog Man?

FLiP FLOP FLiP FLOP FLiP F

I Got an idea!!!

We'll help ya get your job back!!!

Don't worry about a thing!

Just come upstairs...

...and lie down on your bed...

...and I'll read you a bedtime story!

We had a dream but it wasn't scary.

Look at us. We are on the world.

Do you like Dog Man? We Do.

Meanwhile, in another part of town...

...Someone **else** was hard at work, too.

If I can just connect these tubes to the hyper drive...

...then my newest invention will be—

Itsy bitsy spider...

...went up the water spout!

AT LAST!!!

Check out my very latest invention: THE MiGHTY MOTOR BRAiN!!!

HWA-WHAAA

Are ya ready to test it ???

Why do you have to be so **mean**, Grampa?

Guinea pig?

Certainly! The Motor Brain has never been tested!

It might be DANGEROUS!

That's why I need to try it out on **YOU!**

PLOP!

B-But, Grampa, is this thing **SAFE?**

Aw, don't worry, Big Jim. I'll be **fine!**

58

Now let's turn this baby on!

click

Putt Putt Putt Putt

What is it supposed to do, Grampa?

It's a **PERSONALITY AMPLIFIER!!!**

It takes your own innermost psyche...

...And **MULTIPLIES** it **EXPONENTIALLY!**

"Snug Flip, but Snug No Rip!"

Left hand here.

Right Thumb here.

CHAPTER 4

The DOG in The HAT

Meanwhile...

...While Dog Man was still sound asleep...

Z Z Z Z Z

...Li'l Petey and 80-HD were upstairs in the ballroom completing their newest invention.

Okay, 80-HD. Let's test it out!

cLick

meow

Hsssss!

click

Now for the final test!

Wake up, Dog Man!

FLIP FLOP FLIP FLOP FLIP

Me and 80-HD made a new invention!!!

Let's try it on!

PLOP

COOL!

You look just like a cat, Dog Man!!!

And if you press your right ear...

...you can **TALK** like a cat!!!

meow

click

Now try your **OTHER** ear!!!

click

Hsssss!

Now we just need one last detail!

I'm

I'm a cat

I'm a cat.

Perfect!

STOP iT!

NOT Everybody Likes to Be Petted And SLOBBERed on, YA Know!

Sorry, Papa!

Look, it's okay if **YOU** do it. But...

What's **HiS** Problem?

73

That's DoG MaN!

I KNOW iT'S DOG MAN!

WHY's he dressed up Like ThaT???

I'm a.

Oh! 'Cuz he got fired last night...

I'm a.

...and Chief isn't allowed to hire dogs anymore!!!

74

So we turned him into a **CAT!**

NOBODY is going to believe that **HE** is a **CAT!**

They won't?

NO! He looks **RIDICULOUS!**

I'm a cat.

But we **GOTTA** help him, Papa!

Alright, alright...

... Here's some **ADVICE:**

75

Don't roll in any dead fish...

...And QUIT STICKIN' YOUR TONGUE OUT!!!

Wow! He looks better already!!!

Problem SOLVED!

Alright, kid! Let's go get some gelato!

Okay!

Bye-bye, Dog Man! Good Luck!!!

CHAPTER 5

A Buncha Stuff That Happened Next

Soon...

Knock Knock

CRASH!

HEY!

PLOP!

I'm a cat.

meow meow meow me

chief

click click click click

IS it YOU?

But, Dog Man, You can't be here!!!

If Mayor ever finds out...

Hey, Chief! Mayor is here!

PLOP!

Shhhh!

Why is it so **DAMP** in here?

Well, uh— You see, we, umm— uhhh...

Never mind that!

Have you found a Replacement for Dog Man yet?

Well Gee whiz, Mayor. We've only—

What about **him**?

A cat-headed Man would be **Perfect!**

So clean... so smart...

And he has **Nine Lives!**

We should hire _him_!

Well... okay!

AWESOME!

I think I have Dog Man's old badge in my pocket!

Aah! Here it is!

Well look at that!

It fits **Perfectly!**

Meanwhile...

How's the gelato?

Good.

HEY! I started building a new robot this weekend!

I could really use your help this week!

I can't.

Why not?

I'm meeting with my **COMIC CLUB** this week!!!

Look! **ROBOTS** are more **IMPORTANT** than Comics!!!

Why?

Because we **NEED** Robots for Protection!

Why?

Because **GRAMPA** might escape from Jail again!

Why?

Because he's an **EVIL VILLAIN!**

Why?

Meanwhile...

I can't believe my Good fortune!!!

CUPCAKES SAVE LIVES!

This place has EVERYTHING...

CUPCAKE Exit

... including an escape Door!!!

Tee-Hee!!!

cupcake entrance

Now I just need ONE LAST THING!

CHAPTER 6

THE INCORRIGIBLE CRUD

By George Beard and Harold Hutchins

But you can't just forgive **EVERYBODY!**

Why not?

Because some folks don't **DESERVE** it!

Like your **Grampa!**

Oh, I forgave Grampa a long time ago!

How could you forgive that guy?

He **Kidnapped** you!

He left you in a Recycle bin!

He's betrayed You every chance he's gotten!

WHAT kind OF A MONSTER

Hey, Papa, Look!

I caught a worm.

ARE YOU EVEN Listening?

Meanwhile...

Good evening, folks!

I'm Sarah Hatoff with the News!

A weird spider-like cat is busting up the city!!!

CRUD STEAL!

$

Tell us, MR. CRUD: What's it like being a Ruthless villain?

$Hmmm...

Hey, Papa...

How come I met my Grampa...

...but I never met my **GRAMMA?**

Meanwhile... Me Guess me act so **BAD** because me feel so **SAD!**

Hey! Maybe if you find yourself a **BUDDY...**

...You'll become **ENLIGHTENED!**

But where crud **FIND** Buddy?

It not like Buddy Just appear out of **NOWHERE!!!**

CRUD AND BUDDY DO CRIMES!

BUT WHAT CRIME WE DO FIRST?

ME KNOW! US SMASH BOOKSHOP!

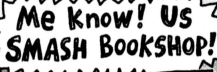

Bertha's BOOKS

C'mon, BUDDY!!!

HEY! CRUD STUCK!!

KA-CLICK!

CRUD NO UNDER-STAND!

I'll tell ya what happened, Cruddy!

It looks like you just got BUSTED...

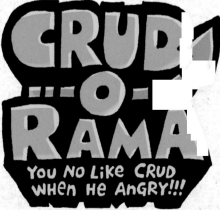

Right
Thumb
here.

And then...

WHAM!

HeY! You're **DOG Man!**

HeY! That's **DOG Man!**

I'm Gonna **HELP** him!!!

I'm Gonna **DESTROY** him!!!

MaYor's House

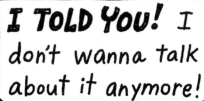

Look— your Grampa...

...He **ABANDONED** me and my mom!

He left when I was just a kitten!

He left when...

He left when my mom was sick.

Your mommy was sick?

Yeah.

She got better, though, right?

Right, Papa?

I don't know, Papa.

Hate has **CAUSED** a lot of problems in this world...

...but it hasn't **SOLVED** one yet.

PETEY & SON

WAiT FoR ME, GANG!!!

NoT So FAST, CHiEF!

DoG Man isn't a cop anymore...

But...

...Yet he was **iMPERSoNATiNG** a **COP!! !!!!**

But...

DoG Man BeLonGs in **JAiL!!!**

But...

And if you help him, **YoU'RE** GoinG to JaiL, too!!!!!

But...

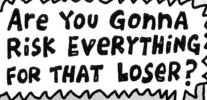

136

CRUD'S MOTOR BRAIN GIVE HIM GOOD IDEA!!!

LiviNG Spray!

Left
hand here.

CRUD READ LABEL CAREFULLY

CRUD SHAKE CAN VIGOROUSLY

CRUD SPRAY BAG THOROUGHLY

Right Thumb here.

CRUD
READ
LABEL
CAREFULLY

CRUD
SHAKE
CAN
VIGOROUSLY

CRUD
SPRAY
BAG
Thoroughly

ME MUNCHY!

150

Meanwhile, at the pond over there...

Okay, class...

Who knows what an **ADVERB** is?

OH! OH! OOH!

Someone **Besides** Melvin this time?

How about you, Molly?

Ummm...

An Adverb is...

it's like... um...

... a word that describes stuff?

Could you be more specific?

Um... you know. Like thingies and stuff?

Please, please, please, pleas, please, pleeeeeeeeeease!

Alright, Melvin.

An adverb is a word or phrase that modifies, quantifies, or qualifies a verb, adjective, or other adverb...

... expressing manner, place, time, frequency...

Okay, thanks! That's great, Melvin.

Now who can use an **ADVERB** in a sentence?

OH! OH! OOH!

Please, Please, Please, Please, Please, Please, Please, Please...

ALRIGHT, Melvin.

Ahem.

I am as SMART as...

...a... a... a...

...A LUNCH BAG!!!

156

Okay, but where's the **ADVERB?**

SNAP

RUN, KIDS, RUN!!!

CHAPTER 10
80-HD POWER

Meanwhile...

PETEY & son

—and now he can barely stand up!!!

I think ya made his head too big.

Oh, **REALLY?** Gee, thanks, **Professor Obvious!!!**

Did ya get your centimeters and millimeters mixed up again?

It's Not Funny!!! I worked Really—

CRASh

BONK

Do you understand
what he's trying
to say?

Not
really.

We can't understand
you, 80-HD!

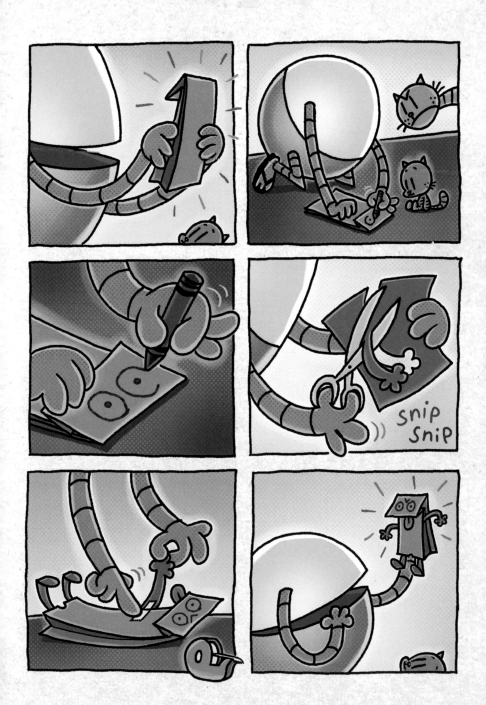

CLACK!

Oh, I get it! 80-HD was tryin' to tell us...

...that a giant lunch bag came to life...

...and our friends are all in trouble!

HE COULD'VE JUST DRAWN A PICTURE!

FLIP FLOP FLIP FLOP FLIP

KA-CLICK

ZOOM

PETEY & Son

Welp, he used the door that time!

SLAP

And So...

Hi, Molly!

Hey, Guys.

What'cha doing?

I'm trying to save Flippy with my Supa Psychokinetic powers...

...but I'm not strong enough.

Maybe **we** can help!

COSTUMES

Oh, I get it!!!

You're "**MR. LOVE**" when everything is going well...

But when something **BAD** happens...

...You suit up and **FiGHT!**

COSTUMES

All he cares about is **Love, Love, Love!**

But when he comes face-to-face with **PURE EVIL...**

...Then the CLAWS COME OUT!!!

See? I **TOLD** ya **HATE** is important!

ONLY HATE can DefeAT HATE!!!

Maybe Wally is right.

Yeah, maybe...

Hey! Let's find out!!!

Are ya ready?

CHAPTER 11

Love vs. Hate
Who Will Win?

Okay, I know **What** we're supposed to do...

...but **HOW** do we do it?

Hmm— that's a Good Question.

Well— what do we **LOVE ???**

You're really good at drawing squids, Molly!

Thanks. I practice all the time!

80-HD loves to draw hearts!

And I Love my Papa, so I'm gonna draw him!

HEY! Don't draw my face on his **BUTT!**

Too Late!

And So...

Psst! Hey Mister...

I Like your new tattoos!!!

They're so cute and darling and Sweet!!!

They make you look **ADORABLE!!!**

Munchy was so embarassed, he let go of Flippy and covered his shame.

Are you okay, Flippy?

I'm fine.

Hey kids! You can stop hiding now!!!

Gee, Mister...

I Love Mustaches!!!

...You're looking LOVELY!!!

You're the most PRECIOUS bad guy I've ever met!!!

I Love Ponies!

Hey, do you wanna Join our COMICS CLUB?

We can all draw Together EVERY DAY!

194

CHAPTER 12

The ULTiMATE Showdown

Me GOT YOUR FRIENDS, PETEY!

Technically, they're not really **MY** friends!

Oh. So You Won't Mind if Me Does...

...THiS!!!

OH, NO!!!

Let's Roll, FLippY!

GRaaampa!

HAW HAW HAW HAW

I can't do it, kid.

I can't Love the way **YOU** Love.

YAY! PETEY BACK FOR MORE PUNISHMENT!!!

Dad...

WHAT?

...I'm done.

DONE WHAT?

Where do you think you're going?

I've gotta get this kid into bed.

WE'RE **NOT** DONE HERE!

Actually, I think we are.

HEY! GET BACK HERE!

G'night, Grampa!

G'night, everybody!!!

Let's all play again tomorrow!!!

Bye, Wally!

CHAPTER 13

THRee Endings

The First Ending
Grampa's Story

HEY!!! COME BACK HERE AND FIGHT!!!

Thanks a **LOT**, MOTOR BRAIN!

You Didn't help me at ALL!

PUNT!

KLUNK KLANK

Hey! My hat!!!

BLONK BLUNK

SQUISH

But then...

ZOOM

DOG MAN! NOOOO!!!

Mayor's House

CRACK MAYOR'S HOUSE CRUMBLE

Chief! NOOOO!

The Third Ending
Li'l Petey's Story

Boy, Grampa sure got mad when you forgave him!

Yeah! If I had known it would bother him so much...

...I would have forgiven him YEARS AGO!

I haven't been here since I was a kid.

It's pretty, right?

Yeah.

Is Gramma in there, Papa?

No.

She's here now...

...And she's here.

Is she here, too, Papa?

Well...

...It's **YOUR** story, kid.

225

HOW 2 DRAW MeLvin The FROG

in **17** Ridiculously easy steps!

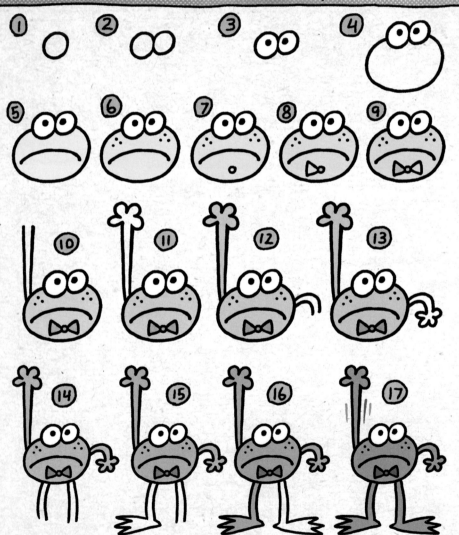

HOW 2 DRAW SARAH

in 18 Ridiculously Easy steps!!!

231

HOW 2 MAKE MUNCHY The Lunch BAG

in **4** Ridiculously easy steps!

Step 1:

Get Supplies:

- ⭐ Lunch bag
- ⭐ Pencil
- ⭐ Tape
- ⭐ Construction paper ⭐ Scissors
- ⭐ Crayons / markers / colored Pencils

STEP 2:

Draw and cut out the arms, Legs, eyes + tongue.

FREE Printable / Colorable template available at: Scholastic.com/catkidcomicclub

STEP 3:

Assemble as shown using tape or glue or paste.

STEP 4:

Take away his evil powers by filling him up with all the people and things you **Love!** Use pencils, crayons, paint, or whatever!!!

WRITE... DRAW... Be CREATIVE!

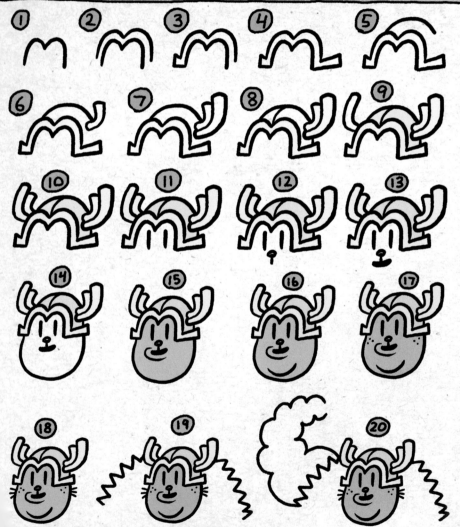

TH DAV PILKEY!

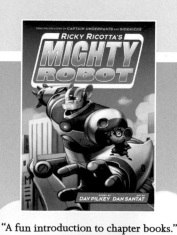

"A fun introduction to chapter books."
— *SCHOOL LIBRARY JOURNAL*

ABOUT THE
AUTHOR-ILLUSTRATOR

When Dav Pilkey was a kid, he was diagnosed with ADHD and dyslexia. Dav was so disruptive in class that his teachers made him sit out in the hallway every day. Luckily, Dav loved to draw and make up stories. He spent his time in the hallway creating his own original comic books — the very first adventures of Dog Man and Captain Underpants.

In college, Dav met a teacher who encouraged him to illustrate and write. He won a national competition in 1986 and the prize was the publication of his first book, WORLD WAR WON. He made many other books before being awarded the 1998 California Young Reader Medal for DOG BREATH, which was published in 1994, and in 1997 he won the Caldecott Honor for THE PAPERBOY.

THE ADVENTURES OF SUPER DIAPER BABY, published in 2002, was the first complete graphic novel spin-off from the Captain Underpants series and appeared at #6 on the USA Today bestseller list for all books, both adult and children's, and was also a New York Times bestseller. It was followed by THE ADVENTURES OF OOK AND GLUK: KUNG FU CAVEMEN FROM THE FUTURE and SUPER DIAPER BABY 2: THE INVASION OF THE POTTY SNATCHERS, both USA Today bestsellers. The unconventional style of these graphic novels is intended to encourage uninhibited creativity in kids.

His stories are semi-autobiographical and explore universal themes that celebrate friendship, tolerance, and the triumph of the good-hearted.

Dav loves to kayak in the Pacific Northwest with his wife.